1

The Golden Road: My Journey with Spirit

ISBN: 9798654351883

THE GOLDEN ROAD:

My Journey with Spirit

BY
BRYONY ROGERS

White birds land on the dawn fields

like punctuation.

Day is beginning.

Introduction

The voice that I 'heard', or more accurately felt and knew inside myself, after the Solar Eclipse in August 1999, 'spoke' to me in a clear, gentle way, and said:

Take strength from your heart.
I am your Golden Road.
Bathe yourself in this Essence.

My heart at this time was opening in a profound way, and I was learning to take strength from it more. I was living in the Findhorn Spiritual community, in Northern Scotland, having followed my intuition and a series of heart encounters to be there. I was experiencing a deep feeling of harmony, peace and connection to all of life and the Universe which lasted for a number of months.

At the Solar Eclipse on August 11th 1999, I experienced a powerful opening and began to receive extended guidance from a Divine source about the Spiritual Truths and the Heightened Reality I was beginning to experience and live. As the sun vanished from view, my body clock turned upside down. My periods came two weeks early, signalling that an unusual cleansing process was taking place and strong direct channellings started to come through me, with no promptings. These continued to come clearly and in volume through to Easter 2000, and this voice and guidance has continued to be available to me ever since whenever I open to the silence, stillness and inner peace that enables it. This is a practice I have learnt and developed more in the years following. This inner voice, and the knowing it brings, is the same connection to the Divine through an inner voice that Eileen Caddy, the founder of Findhorn, heard through her life, that Ghandi, Joan of Arc, Julian of Norwich and so many others have heard through the Centuries, and that is,

I believe, available to us all, when we listen. Eileen Caddy called it 'the still small voice within'.

This book shares some of the guidance I have received, along with what I have learnt and how I have grown from opening to and following, 'The Golden Road'.

TABLE OF CONTENTS

Foreword: Beliefs

Before I go any further, I want to outline some of my beliefs, that have been fundamental to my journey.

➢ The Earth is Sacred

➢ We are of the Earth, and our Lives and Selves are Sacred too.

➢ The Earth is a conscious, living Being.

➢ Nature and everything in it, is a web of living connections; these join us to every other living thing.

➢ Love permeates all life and interconnects us all.

➢ This Web of Light, the living energy body of the earth and life, enables magic and communication to occur between different living beings; animals, spirits, plants.

➢ I have been blessed to tune into, receive and understand some of these communications.

➢ We can all hear and understand if we listen, in silence and with love and respect.

➢ In its highest form the energy of the human being is like a tree, a conduit of light from the heavens to earth, linking the two, linking all that we are and all that we can be.

➢ In this way, as the Human form and Being is evolving and is channelling elevated energies, that can transform us. They might take the form of visions, healing power, understandings, wisdom: we bring the Light to Earth.

➢ With and through these beliefs, I have made a journey which I wish to share. I hope you enjoy and benefit from this sharing. Many blessings.

<u>CHAPTER ONE</u>

i Earlier Years:

Before my experience at Findhorn in 1999, the Inner Voice of the Golden Road had been coming to me for a few years, with odd words and phrases, and occasional visions, such as the powerful vision I had in the Summer of 1997 of a Huge Spirit Eagle formed of White Light, hovering above me as I floated alone, meditating, in a wild woodland river in a remote part of Lancashire.

This beautiful Eagle spoke to me, and said,

Breathe, Trust, You are Held

and energy poured between him and me in a transmission. At that time, I had just learnt that the Eagle carried the Medicine of Great Spirit for Native American Tribes. This was deeply meaningful to me.

This powerful message of the Spirit Eagle continued to come to me in other visions and messages that year. As I was given Reiki by my friend Nadia, in my house in Islington, London, I saw an Angelic figure, in the form of a flower of bright powerful white light. She bent towards me and told me

I will never leave you

Then, at the Winter Solstice, I took part in a ritual with three women friends. We tuned into a deep space of journeying, and I saw myself walking with a bay coloured horse, towards the sun, which was just rising over the edge of a wide plain. I sensed that there would be storms ahead but that I would be OK…….. I had no idea at that time just how bad some of the storms would be. But that Solstice, I heard the words

You are already healed

and I made a commitment to write. I also heard:

Trust me, Hold on tight, and *Love, love, love*

- and experienced a powerful sense of strong and endless Love descending on me and being present with me, leading me on.

I heard:
> *This is the most important thing there is, the work and task*
> *of being real and authentic - don't ever give it up*

This is our vital work

The thing is to trust yourself always, this will carry you through

In these years in the late 1990's, I bought myself a ring, making a commitment to myself and my journey. At this point I had two rings; one, a Celtic pattern, a knot which I think of as 'the still-point at the centre of the moving world', and the other a silver ankh. The ankh (pictured here) is an Egyptian hieroglyphic character symbolizing eternal life. The name means Breath of Life or the Key of the Nile.

The ankh ring broke soon after this, and I gave it to my Mother to return to the shop in which I had bought it - and then, in the following years, I returned to the symbol, joining, and studying with, the Fellowship of Isis for a short while. One night in 1998 I had a powerful dream one night in which I became the Ankh itself, full of light, glowing. I had a strong sense of Isis being with me closely for a number of years, and have continued to feel a connection to Her since. At the Full Moon in Islington, in 1996, I prayed to Isis 'make me whole'. I had my feet on the ground and my heart open. My hands and arms intuitively reached up into the sky. I sensed that She took my hands and pulled me through - up into my new self, passing through fire into water, I am made whole. I heard in my heart and mind a voice which spoke to me and gave me a new name -

Tree

I am Tree.

I made a pledge:

I dedicate myself to life and to my creativity and my love.

I pledge not to betray myself or you, Life, Source of All that Is'

I heard

Conclude and honour the tree

I wrote from the voice of Isis as I felt Her at the time:

Get up girl, get up, life is happening. It has been happening for the longest time. This is the truth. Step in, feel it on your feet, your legs, your thighs, up and over and through there, and then your belly, your back, your chest, neck, head,

All of you, up and over and in - until you are complete and whole in it. New breath. That's the way. Good girl. You're doing fine, just fine. My love. I love you, love you, love you. Yes I do. I always have and I won't ever stop. I love you. Feel the joy of breathing, of living, of loving, of being.

You are beautiful, for you are alive.

In 1998 I also had another deep and profound dream, where I met the Divine Feminine, the Goddess.

She told me:

I have been trying to give you something for a long time. It is healing.

She handed me a stone, and energy pulsated through the stone and into my body.

I asked Her, *what is the priority in my life at the moment?*

She replied, ***The true solution.*** I asked Her to tell me more about this.

17

She said;   *It is God, embodied and made whole.*

It is Goddess, divined in all things.

It is your own true Self, made whole.   In friendship and

enlightenment.'

These are powerful truths, and this dream resonated deeply for me.

At New Year 1999, I learnt about a gathering of International Singers and Sacred voice artists that would be happening in Aberystwyth in Wales at Easter that year. It was called 'The Divinity of the Voice' and I felt strongly called to attend. I had been channelling songs and developing my singing voice since 1997. I put myself down to work at the conference in exchange for free entrance to the event and bought myself a train ticket to travel to Aberystwyth. I had an amazing, profoundly heart-opening week at the festival, learning a lot about the Sacred Voice, and what is possible with its incredible power.

At this gathering, I met a woman who had lived on the small Island of Erraid in Scotland, just off the Isle of Mull, at the outreach community of the Findhorn Community. What she told me about Erraid, and the wild raw nature there, captivated me. I felt a strong calling to travel there, and was also drawn by the idea of joining a community. After speaking with her, I sat on the stone window ledge at the turn of the steps in the large old building we were in, and I cried and cried. My heart had been impacted in a new way and I had found a new sense of coming home.

So I travelled to Erraid and spent a fortnight there in the early Summer of 1999. Erraid is a beautiful island, with rocky undulations and outcrops, surrounded for most of the time by the cold sea. During my stay with the community I dived deep into sacred singing, finding myself nourished and energized by the morning meditation and song session in the sanctuary that overlooks Iona. White sand, grey blue sea, strong colours in the bright sunlight. One night I sat on the rocks and sang to the seals that were scattered on the waters edge. They edged closer, looking at me with their big black round eyes. With me was a young Belgian man, Tom, who I had been spending a lot of the fortnight with. We were travelling deep into personal connection and at the end of my fortnights stay, I made plans to travel to spend time at the main Findhorn Community to stay with him and pursue our relationship.

And so I did. And through that Summer, this relationship and my relationship with Spirit profoundly opened up, until the significant deeper opening of the August Eclipse.

ii The Voice

The phenomenon of 'hearing a voice', or voices, is also, of course, in Western Societies, often pathologised and seen as the symptom of a mental illness. This also happened to me, a number of times, in the years that followed, in times when I was struggling to ground and integrate big expansive energies, and unusual visions, and my experience tipped into spiritual crisis. Though I understand the impulse towards pathologising, and realize that crisis is challenging; I feel much is lost from our society and culture by the reaction of placing labels, constraints and pharmacological suppressants on the visions and spiritual experiences of people when they are sensitive, vulnerable and open, rather than supporting them in processing these experiences.

I see the need for a greater awareness and understanding of this phenomenon, and the resources to support people to process their experiences and come through stronger, and wiser, with important gifts. I am glad to be part of a movement of people advocating for this change.

After one time of Crisis, I heard:

This time has not been in vain.   The conditions of pain and struggle have been intended - Nothing manifests without express purpose within the glory that is my eternal Law of Creation. All is unfolding according to my Divine Wisdom and shall be known and revealed accordingly. It is so and ever shall be; there is no exception to this rule of Divine Law. All that is is manifesting is my creation, the expression of my Divine Will, which is Love-Wisdom.

At the time, I found aspects of this difficult to accept, and felt overwhelmed by my grief at the experiences.

I then heard these healing words:

There is great beauty here in this process of review and recognition of the passageway you have taken, through the dark times and the times of great illumination. There is much that shall be gained from this, a new understanding of yourself and of your place in My Divine embrace.
    Which is eternal, ever-lasting.   (*This is deep and profound).
    You are met in Me, in my Name.

Be peace, Beloved, understand that the workings of your mind and life as it has intercepted with certain other lives the Mental Health System has been very difficult, and density and destruction has been encountered. You have come through this, deeper and wiser than before. You can live anew from this place of deep understanding of human limitations, your own included, the limitations of this

Mental Health system, and the power of the Intense Life force that burns in your Heart.

I also heard this, which could also be relevant for others experiencing crisis:

It is peace, it is peace that is required of you, peace that answers to the Self. You have been ungrounded and not yet integrated great powerful forces of Light and Power, openings you have experienced. You need to prioritise the force field that surrounds you in your healing practices. Chi gung in the garden. Sleeping outside. Connection with the earth outside every day. Connection with Nature everyday.

The integration of the energies after Spiritual opening is a really vital process; and these practices that are suggested here are all effective and powerful tools that support in the healing process of integration. This is a truth I have learnt to recognise more and more as time has progressed. It takes dedication and practice, but it makes all the difference.

Further guidance after crisis:

You are here now.

Here in my Love and the ever-lasting heart that surrounds you, that beats for Life. Find this truth, in the very centre of your being. Your pain is understanding and reflecting grief and loss. You grieve and feel anxious over what has been experienced.
Your perception is what creates your experience within this realm, and all realms. When you perceive isolation, separation and violence – through the experiences you wrote of – and feel emotions of fear, grief and anxiety, without acknowledging

these feelings and perceptions as such, you are opening the door to the manifestation of the physicality of these experiences. You have seen that, at times, you have not been able to step beyond these emotional and energetic experiences and to articulate them to others. To witness yourself beyond them, when they take over in crisis states. Because you have not felt safe to do so. Feeling and articulating your emotions, to yourself, or others, brings clarity and empowerment.

Find the blessing, find a blessing here, now in this moment.
All can grow and change and be made fresh.
All can be remade.

I breathe, and feel:

The blessing of my breath. The blessing of the Sacred music playing on my computer and the little speaker it comes through. The blessing of the feeling of great spaciousness. The blessing of Ben's companionship (my black tom cat). The blessing of having the house to myself and space and time in which to explore. The blessing of the writing and the knowledge that I am held in God's heart, always and eternally.

You are free. Free to learn and choose a better way than this previous pattern, and this is what you have done.

At a later date, I prayed: 'May I connect with the highest source of divine intelligence and healing, knowledge, wisdom'.

I heard:

You are. This connection is always present when you breathe into the silence and the peace.

I breathe and see the power of the Light in myself, a clear channel of energy flowing through.

You have always been thus.

When the Spiritual Guidance started to come to me in great volume in 1999, I wrote it down. I have continued to do this through the years, whenever I have felt called, and feel this is an important aspect of my practice. It has always felt powerful and healing to share it with others. This practice of sharing has developed into the service of channelled songs and mantras, as a healing practice for people, alongside my Reiki, Voice Coaching and Sound Healing offerings. I offer this work in Lancaster, UK, and Otaki Gorge, New Zealand, and through the internet by Skype and audio recordings. You can read more about this work at www.songofawakening.org.uk

The Source I am connecting with through the Voice I hear is deeply healing, it is pure clear Divine energy. I have also connected with many named Beings and Spirits with specific identity over the years. These have included Angelic and non-manifest, highly evolved Spiritual Masters, and Spirits of friends and relatives who have passed over, and have a message to convey. I have also had the experience of connecting with the spirits of people who are still living at times, which has tended to happen when there is a specific personal message to be conveyed. It is an ongoing learning experience for me to sense and discern different energies when they come into focus and move through me.

This has been and is perhaps one of the most important lessons and practices in my life. The greater depth of stillness and silence I am able to access in my meditation and mindful living makes this much clearer and easier and is the central tool for me. Primarily the Voice and energy of guidance that comes to me, when I open to Silence, is the energy of Pure Spirit.

I hear: *Know me as the One, as All things.*

                    I am Mother, Father both.
                    I am within you and all around you.

                    I am the one Voice, and all other voices are mine.
                    I am the one Soul, existing in all Souls.

                    My heart beats in your chest.
                    We breathe as One. Know me as yourself.
                    Let nothing worry you

Be at Peace. You are my divinely beloved daughter, created as a manifestation of my glory. I have placed within your chest a diamond of pure light which transmits my divine energies into this plane through your existence. Your body is a force of Living Light, my fire of Love burning for all to see and know. My blessed daughter you are here to do my work, to take your throne of Divine Light here on earth.. It is my will that you know and understand the nature of your time on earth so far, which has been a particular testing-ground, given by my grace, in preparation for the time to come, when all souls shall quicken towards their union with me. This is the passage through, the gateway, for which mankind has been waiting and

longing. There is only joy to be had in this knowledge of its imminent arrival and that fact that you are here, in this place, on the earth at this time. The result of all your previous incarnations is this Peace and the truth of this knowingness.

As I ask about the Voice, I hear:

There is no call for this excessive labouring to hear my voice – the voice of your people, the tribe of God – we are one eternally. This voice is always there when you open to it, in peace and willingness. You know and recognise us within all that you do, all that you are – we are divine truth eternally expressed; we are, yes, the birdsong in the heavens, the cry of the new-born lamb, the awakening of the earth, of all of life, to the possibilities held in each breath of spring.

The world is made new.

Let yourself be fully Held by Me, as by water, or the birds by the air.

You are finding your voice, seeing yourself more clearly and with a knowing of and beyond the voice, (that I hear) *whilst being Open to it. Do not fear. You are discerning the voices and the energies that are inherent within them. This is an important skill for you in the new world we find ourselves in. Your sensitivity is inherent and deep.*

My spiritual awakening in 1999 changed my life and opened me to Grace and a huge sense of potential in my life.   At that time, I heard:

To your heart, constantly, let the Light shine. Let the Light stream forth unto your brothers and to all souls guided to you.

Let your Light lead the way only. Let the future be revealed in the Light you show the world. It is freedom, joy exceeding known limits.

You are shedding your man-made armour, which is no longer appropriate for the age ahead. Bliss will be known in all you achieve.

Let joy be the watchword for all you do. Let the colours fly, let the joy be known.

Eternal rest in the beloved arms of God.

You have to know the strength of your own spirit, and its endless power.

I would have you know your own strength and know that you can always rest on it, always rely on it. It will not let you down Beloved, nor will it leave you

I also heard:

In each moment the light of God is understood.   In each soul.

This a profound truth and an awareness that I have come back to again and again in my Coaching and teaching work with Heartsong Singing, and in everyday life. I know that as we share in Sacred Song, energy techniques and practices, in the groups I run, in my online one-to-one work, and in the profound silence of Meditation, that each Soul is connecting with their own Divinity. As I support groups and individuals in the journey of opening to their authentic voice and the empowerment and self-knowledge this can bring, I give thanks for the way I am supported in this journey myself.

The angels speak to me now and say

This is central, it is the absolutely vital aspect of your soul's work that is to be shared and maintained with integrity and clear purpose.

This is a journey you have undertaken.
The destination is now.

The understanding is in the silence, the knowingness.
Trust it endlessly. It will never fail you.

CHAPTER TWO

i The Holy Present:

THE PRESENT

And the joy within it;

This is the now you have been dreaming of.

Your destiny is unfolding in the experience of each moment.

You hear the call in the cell of the body and the crease of your fingertip.

You feel what is said in every fibre of your body – how can there be room for doubt or misbelief? The experience is total and it is to be one of peace. The joyful delivery of our words.

Each breath is a new chance for life to flourish, for the energies of my divine love to flow through you – there is nothing you have to do to enforce this – no labouring on your part

It is like this; earthly life is but progress towards the present, which is the eternal now, in my hands.

All life is an expression of Love for me and longing for the completion of the soul's journey; union and total reconciliation with me, which, through my grace and will, and your surrender to the divine plan, you are to be blessed with at last, while on this earth plane.

Your soul knows and rejoices in your imminent arrival at this point of totality of existence and there is to be found much cause for subservience to full understanding of this; take it into your heart as you take food into your mouth and belly and are fed by it.

There is only total nourishment for you, on all levels, at all times, for you are my divine child, in flight now within my ever-lasting love as surely as these birds take the air. All that surrounds you is my Love and there is only nourishment to be

had from it.

All is Peace; this never-ending knowingness, which is total, of my Love for you. Rest in it, beloved daughter and let life come to you, as decreed by me, in full accordance with your soul's knowingness and desire and always for the highest good. Let yourself be fully held by me, as by water, or the birds by the air.

Your soul is in the water of my love, immersed totally, knowing only the delight of oneness and the sanctity of all-that-is.

It shall be so for all my children, in the time of my choosing and as the quickening occurs in each.

ii The Power of the Silence:

Your soul is in the water of my love, immersed totally, knowing only the delight of oneness and the sanctity of all-that-is. It shall be so for all my children……..

Again and again through my life I have reopened to the profound healing that is present in this knowledge of being held by Love, by the Divine, and the space wherein it resides; the Silence. In the Silence of Meditation, I move deep into myself and into connection with All That Is, as it manifests in the Natural world that surrounds me and is available everywhere – through the air, the sky. the soil, the sun on the mountains over the valley, the green of the plants coming up through the black earth.

I sat in my yurt at Middlewood (Lancashire, UK) this morning, early, and listened to the wind blowing in the trees, the birds singing, the regular heartbeat of the wind turbine turning. I watched the shadows of leaves and grasses moving on the white inside of the yurt. I moved deeper into silence, focussing my attention on the very centre of my being - remembering the Pranic Tube that the Hathors spoke of in The Hathor Materials book (Tom Kenyon) that I read recently in New Zealand. I find a profound silence and a powerful energy there at the centre. I felt this energy echoing and growing into the profound Silence that surrounds me in this Natural world. I felt myself dissolve, felt the greenery outside the yurt inside me, living and breathing with me. It is a profound loving embrace.
In this space, I hear:

The silence can be trusted. It is the all that is.
The wonder of the stars is reflected in your alignment,
the surf on the shore, the call of the wolf.

35

Find delight in the depths of silence and see your destiny evolve.
You are fully ordained and the mission now ahead
can be unfolded.

Wait in the silence, wait like the rose waits to open,
in knowingness of God, and its full delivery.

Wait without knowing, trusting.
Wait in the silence, for the dawn.

In each moment the light of God is understood. In each soul.
The understanding is in the silence, the knowingness.
Trust it endlessly. It will never fail you.

The knowing is the surge of the sea in your heart that will never stop.

It is bliss and unending joy. It is in every single moment of your beingness on earth in your true embodiment and light.

There shall be answers known in the silence. There is a song to dance to emanating from your open heart. The silence is held within this song, the truth revealed. Embrace the undiluted kernel seed of life revealed and known in each instant. Know it for what it is, sing it into life, beloved.

CHAPTER THREE

Divine Earth Wisdom:

It is the wisdom of the Earth I am blessed to access, wisdom found in the silence at the heart of the river's current, in the breath of the trees, bending in the wind, in the heartbeat of the hills. All of creation. It is 'from God', from Spirit, from the deepest part of the Earth's being, there in the deepest part of Myself, which is also You.

My understanding of God has shifted and changed over the last twenty years, and is continuing to evolve. It feeds me daily. From a rich understanding of the Goddess in my Twenties, I came to know God as a Father at Findhorn, where I lived in 1999 and 2000. This relationship also contained an understanding of the Christ as Living force, embodied in every single human heart as a powerful potential of Divine Love Wisdom. My connection with God the Father was directly explored through my engagement with Catholicism, when I walked on the Pilgrimage route to Santiago de Compostela in 2003. On this walk, which included visiting many Churches and Cathedrals with much religious iconography, the focus on the martyrdom of the first Christ was profoundly disturbing to me, and led to a sense of imbalance. By 2004, searching for a way to express the Divine balance I intuit is real, I was praying to and with 'Mother-Father God' and much of the guidance shared within these pages comes with this understanding – I heard:

Know that we are one, the mother, the father and the child. Held within the Light of God, the light of the sun rising, held within the Light of your heart, which is a spinning wheel of light, containing all life and galaxies of indescribable wonder. Know that you are chosen for this role and it is part of the path you shall tread on this earth. The role I speak of here is that of understanding this connection, and living it, in awareness.

I also have developed more of an awareness of the Beloved nature of my relationship with the Divine. In more recent years, my sense of the Divine rests in the understanding of the greatest imaginable Creative principle, which is both within and external; this is both the Beloved and the Great Spirit. One of the chants I sing has the lyrics, *'Oh Great Spirit, Sun, Earth, Sky and Sea, You are inside and All around me.'* This force infuses, informs and empowers all life.

However we understand God; the Divine Great Spirit is inside and eternally present in all we see and experience. God is the Perceiving Heart, through which all is known. In 1999, as I mentioned, the healing voice I heard inside me said,

Take strength from your heart.
I am your golden road.
Bathe yourself in this essence.

This healing power of the Heart is not something I have to reach for or to struggle to attain, negating or disowning any part of myself, in any way – rather it is something I breathe into, am embraced by, enfolded by. It is the return to

Myself, to what I am. Present; Living. The Heart is the ultimate and profound connection between all living beings, which delights in the joyful and meaningful dance of existence in which we all partake – and which calls to us to partake in loving consciousness.

I realize now how totally I find myself in that connection, living and dancing with the Spirit of Nature.

CHAPTER FOUR

FORGETTING

Experiencing Struggle and Strife.

I wrote, 'do you feel my pain';
I hear: *it is an illusion, it is separation from God.*

When I found myself in the same place of struggle and wrote, 'why have I put myself in this place again,
– I heard: *to learn the limitations of the ego.*

The purpose of this chaos is to bring to light anger, fear, resentment – to be blessed in the Light.

Embrace the despair, the feeling of having got it wrong – you have not got anything wrong, you have simply not completed the mission. You are still performing. The hollowness inside persists.

The forgetting, and the coming asunder – losing yourself in third dimensional reality – this is a healing which has to happen. Alignment has to be total, anything else is too risky. There is intimacy with God in every single moment, every setting; find it there. This is your responsibility, and also your joy. Patience and more centering is required.

I accept my responsibility. I open to my joy.

Here, now, standing on this shoreline, as the sun rises, I find a new heartbeat in my chest, and a new light in my eyes. You are denying the truth of your evolvement and the nature of your soul path. You are to be calm and in harmony at all times to facilitate the transmission of high frequency energies. This is your nature, this is your role.

As I struggle to verbalise I hear: .. *There is no need to repeat a question in that way – it only creates mental confusion and debris.*

Doubt creates a hole in your energy field through which negativity can enter. It affects the transmission state directly.

Without conscious intent you are closing your own source of life, and drifting in the lower realms. The unconscious intention behind this choice is to delay the process of alignment with the truth; the expression of your truth – it is an ancient testing ground.

The hole doesn't actually exist in dimensional reality, though you allow it to be through your mind and it has a real effect. It exists as lack of trust and is parallel to the pain in your knee, which expresses your choice to walk with hesitancy on the earth. The lower frequencies and entities you invite in as chaos and self-doubt give you nothing in the connection. They feed off you. The purpose of this challenge is to align you more fully in the light with your own truth at this time. It has to be a conscious choice, and you are to see the confusion for what it is; unnecessary for you and totally foreign to your energy field – which is bright clear light.

Do not let fleeting illusions pull you from your path and the quest for knowledge. Trust the words that you find here, in the silence, when I am with you as one.

Know the Light and Truth always as you walk amongst the scattered debris of third-dimensional reality. Do not be tempted by the scars or pain which your brothers exhibit, and which you still carry within your own Christ-heart. Know them for what they are; illusions, broken dreams. The limits of man come up against the truth in the Christ Light in all, endless. Know them for what they are and touch them with your love, from the Source. The tenderness of your sword-fire.

The words I speak in you at this time are passed through fear as you attempt to control that which is not yet in form. In doing this you create the illusion of pain.

The road you could see before you is clear of illusion and pain, there is only love and the blessedness of truth in all things. I am with you, eternally, as are all those who walk in the truth.

There is no call for this excessive labouring to hear my voice – the voice of your people, the tribe of God – we are one eternally.

I ask – why have I been fighting, denying and judging myself?

You have been living within the confines of the ego. Your fear of the surrender to the truth has kept you confined in a mental space. It comes from your past. It is to be released and known for what it is – a stepping stone across to God. Great compassion in this recognition.

You are choosing to experience pain as you test and challenge the limits of your self-deception. Everything I show you is to be accepted with the totality of Love that I am in you.

The 'being blown open' is required for the truth to be fully manifested. You resist this. Resistance creates pain.

These are the limits of the moment; accept them as my Love. They are beyond understanding. But they will change.

And so there is this breath, and then the next. There is this moment, and then the next moment, and there is the opening.

There is the opening into silence, peace, love and awareness. Into possibility.

All is possible.

All can be created, remade, refound. Everything can be seen and held in Love, and turned around, made new.

We are opening.
We are coming through.

THE LOWER WILL

Through the pushing of the lower will, holes appear in the auric field and lower entities can enter at will. It is imperative that you correct these misbalances.

Lower and misguided energies are what are attracted to you at this time. Yes, they feed off your light. You must always ask for support in returning these spirits to the Light.

But more importantly you must correct the state of affairs that enables such an entrance in the first place.

You can do this through sound.

Try to make sound healing a part of your daily ritual. After silent mediation attend to the need of each chakra with the sacred syllables you have learnt. (I use the Jonathan Goldman vowel sounds and the Indian Bija Mantra sacred sounds. Any focussed use of our own voice strengthens and stimulates the auric field. Simply singing or toning vowel sound up the chakras – OO < OH < AH < EY < IH < EE - can strengthen, clear and balance the auric field and the energy body.)

You also need to bathe deeply in silence, the meditation you have recently begun, and the sense of foundation you have found there is imperative to the good work you need to do in preparation for ascension.

You can visualize gold energies of the higher auric fields as smooth unbroken shell. Visualize a perfect protective shell around your aura. Do this regularly throughout the day.

EVERY LIVING THING – PAN

The great God of Nature, Lord and Father of all the Natural world, Pan and I have a relationship that has developed over the years. At Clava Cairns, an ancient burial ground and place of transformation near Findhorn, in 1999, I saw Pan for the first time.

He said, *'Honour all my children'*, and in a vision, the black panther, one of my power animals, stretched and ran, showing her power.

Pan spoke and said: *Every living thing is a child of God, and has a spark of divine light in them. Every living thing is worthy and deserving of love and compassion.*

This includes all of us, every one.

CHAPTER FIVE

Aspects of Awakening

DIVINE BLESSING - We are Held

You are held as this bird is held; there is no need for effort, all is brought to you, as an expression of my unending Love for you. There is no desire necessary as all is manifested instantly in the oneness that-is-all. Rest in this dear daughter, be at peace.

You are held in my arms eternally as one and all is well. I am always with you; we never part. All is one, eternal, in the sanctity of bliss and the soul's union with me.

These are the words spoken by me on this day to reassure you and quicken your resolve to relax into the truth that is your soul's understanding. To never be parted from me, to breathe as one in the wholeness of this Divine Soul embodiment that is your self on this earthly plane.

In eternal Love

I am never away from you dear daughter, nor you from me, we are one, merged eternally.

You shall embody and be known as Love-Wisdom, the truth that is Love.
In your heart is the eternally transforming centre of Peace, which is truth revealed in the essence of your beingness on this place. Embody the wisdom of your heart by breath and silence within, where indeed you know your greatest

truth, that which you are. I am always with you. You have been chosen, in countless lifetimes, to walk the way of truth with me. You have never deserted me or turned knowingly from me. You are at the centre / heart of those who walk this plane in my name; it is eternal honour that you have gained through your faithful service.

It is only Love my child, that brings you to me, and it is only Love with which I receive you, eternally in my arms.

You are always held here, known and recognised in the true light of your soul; that which is to be manifested fully on this plane as the key role of this lifetime. All that manifests through you shall be as I desire – for the plan created, by my will, for the restoration of the Light onto the Earth.

It is only through your Love that my Love can be known – there is nothing else required.

Countless souls require the nourishment and have chosen, that which I will manifest through your open heart, soul-embodiment. It is truly your life's work to know this as truth and watch as miracles unfold.

Relax into my arms and understand – nothing will be asked of you that is not wholly of Love.

There is only Love – this truth you know. Watch and observe as it filters through your consciousness like clear water, or my skies, in the coming days. Let it unfold into the morning that is now, as a flower unfolds itself in my light, until it fills you totally. Let Love fill you.

There is only now; an eternally present expression of bliss manifesting as growth into fullness-in-Me. This is all there is, this Love.

You are yourself LOVE, an embodiment of the divine source of all that is. And it is to be expressed. This is the will of God. It is the plan, to be fulfilled.

Your alignment is total and you must now choose to live accordingly in the trust that this great truth deserves. Nothing is left behind, and there is never any cause of lack or want. You are my child and my will is expressed through you.

You lose the connection when you enter into fantasies, memories, mind-games. Enter, with me, the clear space of this light, this total understanding.

This is where the adventure starts.

Your knowledge of my beingness is deep – a river of truth flowing deep and wild. It is not to be dammed. Let it flow. Let your wildness live, in your song, your shout. You are an emissary of light, part of the brotherhood, the network. Forever recognised.

You are my river bank, my pipe on which I play perfect peace. You hold the endless flow of laughter and joy, my poetry of all emotion. You are my firebird, carrying the truth of my endless love in your flight, your rise and fall on the wings of endless freedom. You are my pen, with which I write the words of my knowing, the truth which rises endlessly in all hearts, in all creation. You are my voice with which I sing in endless Love. My endless creation, my endless love, expressed in all you say and do and are, with no exceptions, my endless One.

You are returned beloved. You are complete in me, the entirety of my creation. You are whole in me for the glory of my name. Let the glory of All that is sing forth. Let yourself sing dear daughter. Let your body be healed in the water of my love for you which surrounds you now even as that amniotic fluid which held you before you were born into this life. Let yourself breathe in the truth of my love for you; it is all around you. It is in everything.

These are my words to you, my breath in you, my love is never-ending. You are held. This is even as the river flows, the truth of your surrender to me – it is given.

Your surrender unto this life and what is chosen for it is now progressing.

It is given dear daughter, let there be no doubt in your mind. You are fully surrendered unto me.

There is no judgement, nothing which needs correcting. What is progressing is your understanding of your role and that which it encompasses within this sphere of existence. Take it all in your stride working in God's name, held in the light.

This is eternal, it cannot be lost. You can never be separated from who and what you are, in the sanctity of God's house, where you dwell forever, held in my eternal embrace.

It is indeed a myriad of voices, of support and reassurance which you hear at this time. We are all present, beloved sister, your tribe, your homecoming is sweet. The longing we have to be united is sweet.

Your heart is sweet. Remain in contact, we need each other. We are on this journey together. You are not alone – you are held within OUR light, our group soul over-lights all that you experience. It is the oneness you encounter at this time of revival.

After a very scary experience in a mental hospital I heard the following reassurance;

The connection is not broken. The web – my eternal creation – is not lost. You are not torn asunder from any of God's children, my child, my child.

Remember this – nothing is lost, you are not lost, you are one within God's eternal creation, endlessly being created anew.

SURRENDER:

In 1999, at the time of my awakening, I heard:

You stand at the gateway to a tunnel of light. The tunnel is Surrender. It leads to union with All-That-Is; the peace of your soul embodiment in this lifetime. You are the gate-keeper. You reside in Peace and have travelled this tunnel over the last years in your time-frame. The Light of your heart, the Christ Within, is Infinite.

This is the work allotted you in this lifetime – to hold the peace of God within your heart that it might radiate outwards. Your role is simply this – to reside in your consciousness, to be. All else is manifested through you as I bring souls closer to the full union they desire and have chosen.

It is the glory manifest as peace and oneness experienced at the river just now that is your role; that of full beingness in harmony with the all-that-is. All else will manifest outwards through you from me. Reside in the peace, know again the renewal and true joy it brings – oneness with me, all things.

That which is outwardly manifested to you at this time is the result of your soul's choosing. Let your consciousness unfold at the time of your soul's choosing, let all be revealed.

All shall be revealed and the truth made manifest in my name, for the good of all. All is well, dear child.

Burn bright with it – the truth revealed, known in an instant. The challenge now lies in accepting what is, with open arms and heart; embrace. Surrender with a glad heart to that which is given by the Grace of God.

Take heed to only align yourself with Spirit and to honour your true nature, which is revealed and known and held within the arms of the one true Brotherhood.

Open further to the unknown mystery that is bliss springing each moment from the heart of God, to whom you are eternally wedded, always as one.

***Surrender** is endless and ever-deepening. It is the act of finding your soul anew in the beauty of each morning.*

This hurdle, surrender, is part of your path at this time. It is not for intellectual games or superficial understanding – as you know. It is to be lived; in the true glory of the soul emissary of God, the divine essence of all-that-is alive in you here now, always.

There is much work to be done as the energy of surrender progresses through your soul embodiment. It is to be lived in each second and it (joy undiscovered) is to be known in full. This is the bringing of the light to earth. It is the work of divine union. It is truly blessed.

The movement you witness around you amongst your brothers and sisters is the momentous shift experienced within at this time. Hold your faith firm. Know you are held.

I saw and felt the joy of the new and total adventure, wings unfolding.

BLESSINGS

At my time living at Findhorn Community, I was giving many healings, or blessings – when I was asked to by Spirit. These worked by me channelling healing energy through my hands, to the crown chakra mostly. In a very similar way to Reiki, which I have more recently been attuned to, and which is strengthened and deepened in my practice of it, by these initial trainings and experiences.. They were very joyous occasions, with the recipient feeling deep peace and contentment. I was mostly working with angelic energies in these blessings, many of them being initiated by Archangel Michael or Raphael.

Then I had one amazing experience of channelling through the energy of dolphins and wolves, to a friend who had a particular affinity with these animals. There was an incredible powerful energy as the spirits of the animals filled the room. It was a profoundly strong presence, joyful and free, which commanded great respect. It was channelled deep into the soul; carrying my friend home, keeping her safe – the Wolf was the guardian of the healing, standing beside her.

The blessings were, on one level, a logical continuation of the spiritual healing training which I had begun in London with the National Federation of Spiritual Healers in 1997 - and completed in 2004. During this particular time at Findhorn in 1999 – for three months, August to December – I was having many dreams of being a healer, and also a medium; meeting with other healers and mediums in the dreams. I see the dreams acting as a kind of training or further initiation, and all this fed into my Reiki training in 2014.

I was told;

It is a very specific task you are performing with each blessing. The energy is always in a state of flux and transmission depends upon each factor, of which you are an element, a part. All is to be held in balance, in joyful anticipation of the

61

return of the light, the knowledge of all that is, working in and through you, and in all your brothers and sisters, in all living things.

Let the gentleness come through, a great wave of compassion, washing the gates of this place, and of your heart.   Let your hunger be satiated. Drink anew and deep on the waters of our love for you – never let your faith waver. We are always here for you, and ever shall be, unendingly

CHILDREN

In 2000 I was also working with the children at the playgroup as part of my work for the Findhorn Community. I loved the work; embracing the passion and wildness of the children. I remember one little boy struggling up a rope, climbing up to the moon. And when he reached the top of that rope and arrived at the moon, he found a terrible monster, but it was one he could overcome.

The playgroup was seen as 'a sanctuary from the adult world' and I was given the following advice on my work;

The children see clearly the light in your eyes. You are to understand your role as helper, keeper, guardian. You are to impart information and wisdom as asked only. Be in the absolutely clear naked truth with them. Hide nothing from their eyes; the little ones who know their freedom. They will bless the adults in turn. The light will radiate outwards.

Seeing the truth in the heart and eyes of the children who share our lives, in whatever relationship, is vital. Children need upholding and honouring for themselves, as we all do, and then we can learn from their unique perspectives and fresh wisdom.

INVERURIE 1999

Inverurie is located on the road between Forres and Aberdeen in Scotland. I was guided to drive there and told I would undertake a series of blessings while there. I was told

By the power of the sword given you at Inverurie, you will cut free from your past.

At Inverurie, after a powerful guided ritual with the stone circle, when the stones spoke to me, and welcomed me in my new life, I was told;

Inverurie is an ancient centre of light. The work you have undertaken will activate the three sites – There are three other stone circles lying in the hills on this road to Aberdeen, each powerful in its own way.

As I slept in my car beside the first stone circle, I received a blessing from Shiva, and saw and experienced the light of Shiva, green, gold and black. 'Black coming from the ground, swirling into green and Gold. The words; *Ye netta Oni, Ma sa ha* filled my mind. The colours and the energy came in from above, filled me, expanded me. My heart was dancing, on fire.

Ye netta Oni, Ma Sa ha – Have Faith in the One.

Inverurie was really my initiation; My blessing, Like the baby in the circle and her mother, who I met, were blessed. The initiation of following the instructions I was given, trusting them, and watching them unfold magically, in wonder – I was told to simply go to the circle, that I would meet someone and would be given somewhere to stay. I met a young woman and her three month old baby girl, in the circle. I had a blessing for the baby, and the woman and I became friendly. She offered me somewhere to stay for the second night of my visit, and introduced me to another woman who became active in helping me to work with and maintain the energies in the stone circles.

It was a very powerful two days of earth ritual and connection. After my blessing at Inverurie the following came through;

Beloved Daughter; it is through my hands and the clarity of your own intention that you have been blessed this day. You are surrendered unto me. The union is complete and can never be severed. You have been blessed with memory. You have walked this earth plane through many lifetimes to earn the honour of true service, the surrendering of the whole that full embodiment of divine presence can manifest.

It is desired that you refrain from searching for answers to questions that arise in the energy of doubt. There is no need for doubt. You are truth revealed.

And then, as I embraced the stones in the circle, the final stone spoke to me;

You have given me love and true recognition. You have touched me with your sword and you will touch others in turn. You will open hearts and doors with the key of true recognition of the divine essence of all that is. Know that we are one and that I am always with you. The moment of our union is eternal.

You carry me with you and I hold you always in the palm of my heart. I am God in all things, know me as such. I am truth revealed. I am in all things, in an eternal oneness of bliss.

*Rest **within** this knowledge. Let it carry you in total peace. This peace is our gift to you.*

Sanctuary.

I was told,

you are working with energies brought to this plane for the express purpose of the fulfilment of the Divine Plan for the restoration of the Earth.

This continued;

You have returned to be made whole in the full conscious knowledge of yourself and the choices you have made. You have returned and are reborn

The struggle is over.

You are known anew and you are coming to know yourself.

     You do well my child to know you are held in my arms. You are uncovering yourself, with my assistance.

     This is a time of recompense. You feel great weariness and the work is heavy and slow. Stay with it and we will lead you through. Follow the light as it leads you. You are coming undone and coming into yourself. Do not let go of this. The road ahead is clear and the way is marked. Let it unfold itself.

     Do not give undue consideration to its form; know that it is always for the best, for we are working with you. The light is with you, and in everything you do. There can be no mistakes'.

Let it be understood that these words in you are as gifts of light for the glory of God, in honour of life, and are to be celebrated.

From doubt towards believing – gather everything that happens, trivialities included, without reservation, regret or nostalgia, in inexhaustible wonder.

Set out forward, one step at a time, from doubt towards faith, not worrying about the impossible ahead.

Light fire, even with the thorns that tear you.

ARCHANGEL MICHAEL

Michael's sword was given to me in a meditation in the sanctuary. This was confirmed numerous times.

My sword is within your heart dear sister, placed there, by the grace of God, towards your surrender and the glory of the One.

The plan is being revealed in everything you say and do. Do not hesitate. The sword is in your hand. You are initiate. Have no fear.

You have demonstrated yourself before and are to have no fear of failure. You are beloved daughter of Christ. Relax and let the light enter fully where it belongs.

Know your own light is multiplied by thousands as you hold the sword. Hold it in your right hand, point down. Know that you are blessed in this. The sword is also the pen; do not let it rest.

It is like this; earthly life is but progress towards the Present, which is the eternal Now

Each breath is a new chance for life to flourish, for the energies of Divine love to flow through you – there is nothing you have to do to enforce this – no labouring on your part.

There is such love surrounding me as I write these words. I feel Michael's Loving presence.

The sword is part of you. You carry it within you and are blessed by it, anointed; you always carry its mark, radiate its blessed light. As you move amongst others they know this. You have earned the right through countless lifetimes of dedicated service.

Michael speaks in and to and through you with these words. It is surrendered. It is given (Essene). All is well

You are blessed in this work sister, as are those who travel alongside you. All shall be reborn. The light shall be known in it's fullest glory. It is as has been decreed. You are reborn. The work is begun. Go in Peace; you carry the sword of Michael within you always.

Surrender and live anew, reborn.

I was told:

You are not working in vain, but with full guidance.

We are united, rest in this. Know it is eternal and endless. Our wings are spread and it – the bird of the soul – is in full flight. Let your will be united and harmonious for the good of the whole.

You will be asked to transform your living experience totally. Nothing is to be expected – only hold to the peace and harmony and stillness.

It is imperative that you keep the harmony of your soul. It is imperative for our mission. You are holding a network of light in your centre. Every time you bring disharmony in and follow doubt or chaos, instead of clear joy, you tear the fabric of the light body.

I hear:

This is the truth of inception of the highest order of Love wisdom, known in your heart and life at this time. It is blessed, and it is the rock on which your whole life is based. Before this time it was implied and growing, known at times; since this time it has been a stable place of knowing that you return to again and again for nourishment. Many lessons have been brought to it's Light.

Know yourself to be blessed.

The future is secured. The way is known.

AZRAEL

Azrael, who identified himself as my Guardian Angel, was one of the first beings of light who introduced himself clearly to me, as a separate and distinct energy. I called on my Guardian Angel to introduce himself in the Chalice Well gardens in Glastonbury.

I later found out that his role is as the angel of death and judgement in Christian understanding, but when he introduced himself I saw lots of stars and sensed a huge, starry body, and I wrote in my journal that he was 'an angel of Joy'. This dichotomy is like that which is contained within the Rune, Wunjo, which is both the rune of death and the underworld, and the rune of bliss. The dancing joy and liberation of death, and judgement or choice that is release from the idea and fear of judgement.

He told me:

You were born to do this work, to carry your light to the darkest spaces.

Walk the path of truth and silence.

Be patient, and Play.

He advised me: *Love and embrace the part of you that feels worthless. Dance her in Joy and abundance, show her the truth. The Light is strong in you and these things are as dried leaves.*

The truth is simple indeed.

Your words are to be spoken with ease, forgiveness and joy – grieving is spent, over now. Know this lightness inside, that holds the truth – and follow it.

DA-BEN

Da-Ben is a guide who works with – to help people develop as Channels; When I connected with him, I heard

'I am an ascended soul, who has served on earth three times, and chosen to assist in this manner at this time.

I have been with you from the beginning. There is much to be understood and brought to rest. Know that I walk alongside you as the journey unfolds.

I am here to ensure that your soul purpose alignment is maintained.

I am with you and would desire you to know this. Know indeed that your heart is full to over-flowing and you have found peace. This is your natural state and it is desirous that it remains.

Capture and transmit these words and feed them to the hungry souls who block their own ears and choose to deny their own light in God, their own truth of knowing. For we are all held, there is no exception, in the light which emanates now from your chest – and from the chest of man - Christ light.

Find the Light within and bring it into the open. Share it without ceasing for it is divine fire and it shall not be dimmed. Indeed it will burn ever brighter, fanned by the ardent need of the listening heart. The truth is known, in your heart, in the words that fall from your mouth, and in all those who hear.

Publish these words.

It is endless dear one.   My protection is total, all it needs is your total trust.

DIMENSIONS / TIMEFRAMES

Within the framework of different spheres of existence exist intricate hierarchies of noble birth. Masters who have descended to earth timeframe such as those known as St Germain and the Christ, exist within the fifth dimension which consists of your Light brothers ascended from the earth plane.

Within these frames of experience the totality of All is manifested in ways that can be revisited in the form of travel known as dreaming whilst you are incarnated on this plane.

You are shortly to return to these levels in this manner and will understand more fully the nature of the journey you have undertaken in this incarnation. You are here in this body to bring my Light to Earth in all you do, and as you progress further the wonders of this chosen journey will become apparent.

For now,

rest in what you are; a part within the whole, blessed with the knowledge of the sanctity of this.

There is no other way to your heart's desire than this union of heart and mind with the soul essence that is Me and all your brothers and sisters. We are as one. It is ordained. We are to be together eternally, as one.

Know that you are held in balance, and that the light does not go astray, is not to be lost.

NEW CHAKRA SYSTEM

Received 2008

The twelve chakra system is the new way; the new model for human kind. The energies of new alignment and truth are being brought forth into your system. They are indeed galactic and universal energies, and must be preserved, in the forms you have found.

The 12 chakras inculcate more light into your system. They spread and navigate that light around a wider arena than previously possible. They are a great step forward in the potential of the divinely awakened human. They are the store house of divine energy – they are the map of the new era. They are the next step - everything we expected and have been waiting for.

You currently carry these new energies in your upper bodies – seventh, eighth, ninth. Beloved, these energies must disperse right through your system, through all the lower bodies and fully into the physical form. This will enable full embodiment.

Time and again we have spoken of the new form, which is to penetrate and affect even the cellular level. This is to be celebrated, as it comes to pass.

The term light-body is an accurate description of the upper energetic bodies being formed during the process of ascension.

Breathe into the earth, through the souls of the feet.

<u>FATE</u>

Know that nothing is pre-written in your terms.

There is no fate in the terms you used to understand it, but fate, in terms of karmic cause and effect exists very properly in this realm, and in all realms.

FLOW OF LIFE

What worked for you in the past, what was true even a week, a day, an hour ago – is not necessarily so now.

Form and meaning is in constant flux as life moves through. To surrender to this brings great freedom and openness.

CHAPTER SIX

LOVE

Love beyond the limits of Time. Love beyond the limits of the alter ego. Beyond the limits of the Self.

Open your heart and your mind, and the Way will become clear.

Follow the love that is in your Heart. The body of Light that surrounds you is the Mother. The body is Love, endless.

There is no judgement, only Love, the perfection of my Grace. All my Children are united in this, held as one. There is no status in Love, only Truth, within which all are one.

Your soul is endless infolded love.

The universe is always supporting you.

This is very powerful for me to read now, as I have realized that I have judgement inside me - and that it is a learned habit and pattern of coping that I employ when I feel vulnerable.

Later I hear:

This understanding is Divine Love expressed. It is All.

Nothing is undone by it, nor shall it be. Refrain from your judgements, your narrowness of perception. But hold yourself in compassion if they occur. This understanding is Divine Fire and is blessed.

No explanations are needed nor apologies. All is in hand. Know that God laughs and Loves in you, in your joy. Love is your abundance.

Come from your own heart in your own now.

Feast upon yourself and upon one another, through the eyes of God. Go bountifully with tidings of love unto the earth. Feed the earth with your love. Give forth a feast of God and you shall indeed be giving forth the harmony of the world.

You are truly loved.

Your grandeur is indescribable.

Live in Love; live it now, in wonder and praise for the glory of the Great I AM, all that you are, expressed in thought and deed. Become all you can be.

All life is an expression of Love for me and longing for the completion of the soul's journey; union and total reconciliation with Me, which, through my grace and will, and your surrender to the divine plan, you are to blessed with at last, while on this earth plane. Your soul knows and rejoices in your imminent arrival at this point of totality of existence and there is to be found much cause for subservience to full understanding of this; take it into your heart as you take food into your mouth and belly and are fed by it.

`There is only total nourishment for you on all levels, at all times, for you are my divine child, in flight now within my ever-lasting love as surely as these birds take the air.

All that surrounds you is my Love and there is only nourishment to be had from it. All is Peace; this never-ending knowingness, which is total, of my Love for you. Rest in it, beloved daughter and let life come to you, as decreed by me, in full accordance with your soul's knowingness and desire and always for the highest good. Let yourself be fully held by me, as by water, or the birds by the air. Your soul is in the water of my love, immersed totally, knowing only the delight of oneness and the sanctity of all-that-is. It shall be so for all my children, in the time of my choosing and the quickening occurs in each.

I saw myself gathered in huge angelic arms of light and carried forwards out into the day and into action, in Love and faith, in the Name of the One.

I am with you child and all my wishes are fulfilled in you and all that you do. Be not assured by falsities or fantasies.

A song came to me:

> Take flight, on the winds
> That are blowing today.   They are blowing
> Out of darkness, into Light and Joy
> They are blowing, out of darkness,
> Into Light and Joy.
> Open the wings of your heart, and know
> That Love will carry you Home
> Love will carry you Home.
> Love is an Endless Sky.

DETACHMENT

It is desirable for your soul's growth and expansion as an expression of love that you refrain from all attachments within this sphere of existence.

It weakens your connection with the Divine which is inherent in all things and with which you are blessed.

You are here to fulfil a purpose of your soul's choosing – and for which you will be supported in all ways.

Freedom is that purpose, and becoming the total whole of yourself in this realm. All is coming to you, for the fulfilment of the plan and the strengthening of my will, for the glory of all.

Detachment is an act of love, clarity and trust.

Let your magnificence shine; it is for the glory of all.

A Love song came to me, describing my relationship to the divine voice that I felt myself connecting with.

The deeper I move into you
The more I know my Love.
Your heart is an endless ocean
Its waters surround me

As the day unfolds and becomes itself
And the light breaks on the sea
I unfold myself into your arms
And becomes the light that is me.

I unfold myself into your arms
In the silence before the dawn
And know that the truth of your endless love
Is where I shall ever be born.

Inside me turns a catherine wheel
Whole galaxies of stars
And the sun and the moon dance endlessly
In the space that is my heart.

I could reach and feel your endless Love
Except that it is my own
And as I breathe in deeper and become myself
This is all I have ever known.

Your heart is always with me
Around, within, above
And all that I encounter
is the touch of your endless Love

Know yourself in the Love you feel
Surrender to its grace
Find yourself and all that is real
In the mirror of Love's true face.

RELATIONSHIPS

Azrael spoke of relationships and said;

It is to be understood between you that Divine Freedom is the only imperative; this is the expression of your souls deepest Love - for God. The Light is there between you. Let it rest, unfold in its own time.

Live and celebrate, the story of both your lives, and the colour in between.

*My presence is all understanding. Your will magnified. Do not judge or taint your knowing with the paintbrush of old. The light burns ever brighter and will continue to do so. (*image of a flame burning up black soot; transmuting all heavinesses, all that holds back, into clear air, into light*)*

Let it be understood; you are ready and your soul is ripe for the seeds of knowledge sprouting. Let this be your will; to find ever clearer, ever simpler access to Me, You carry me with you, it is understood.

I write in your hands, your fingers, your heart. Be blessed and know with the truth of the One that you are always with me. Known and held. We are together.

Trust the words that you find here, in the silence, when I am with you as one.

THE GOD-NOTE

Your heart is opening wide

You are here for this Light-Journey, in the company of your brothers and sisters and my words. Your strength is in the silence and in the Peace, all is uncovered here. Go in Peace and always in Peace. Carry harmony within you. Remember it is yourself.

*You are always whole in me. You are of the Light and you know your own particular **note** – let it RESONATE in all that will come to be, all that unfolds.*

I ask: tell me more about that note -
I see energy vibrating purple and violet.

This is your note, your own unique energy and vibration. When you sound this, though resonance and alignment with the Source, as you encounter it in others and in your life experience, as you did in Nature with the tree this afternoon, in your heart centred song, deeply in your song, this is the energy that is expressed, the vibration that sounds forth in the universe. It is a healing force, and is recognised and responded to by open hearts, and souls.

It is my will that you carry this space and silence within you – and that you know your true self. The space and the silence are where the god-note sounds. This is for the good of all. Let it unfold in this way. Keep your peace. Let my blessings rain down and let the silence in, increasingly.

It is that ocean of peace, unending, huge. I feel it now in the silence of the evening, here on this winter night. The wind blowing outside, my breath sounding in my lungs, my heart beating with recognition and true awareness.

The Peace is never-ending. It is your natural state.

Here is where your true harmony lies and the nature of your own vibration of the god-note can sound most clearly. It is desired that you remain in the silence and carry the Peace within you at all times.

Know only this my beloved daughter – that we (the Light force) are always with you, and that we are one in the Light that is God. All is revealed. All is Provided. There is never any cause for lack.

I asked about this, about how this fits with poverty and famine in the world:

All is provided. You will be blessed in this, if you know where to look. There is much disease in the human state of being, and the collective mind. Damage has been done to humanity. Inequality and unhealthy power dynamics exist in many places. This damage exists, and the gaping wounds that many of my children are living within at this time causes pain.

I feel that pain. I feel an enormous compassion for those suffering in famine and those suffering in war and disaster.

It is a sense of waiting.

We are born to recognise and be aware of the inequality and unhealthy relationships that are in existence in this plane, and to act with responsibility to not

90

perpetuate these, for example buying clothes from fair trade and humane sources, and eating sustainably, to bring these situations to an end as much as we can, and also, in the same hand, we are to be aware of our personal needs, and compassionate towards ourselves.

See the relationships you exist within, and see also the whole interdependence of the world, of all the cultures and societies – for you are one people, living on one planet. You are all born to recognise your connection with your neighbours and also your environment and to live with that awareness in the fullest way you can. You can be free. You can live beyond power imbalances. Do not feel imprisoned by the limits of your society and those who are in power. See their limitations, and see them from a larger place, a more open heart. Feel the beat of your neighbours heart. Reach out and connect where you can.

The voice that I hear and the energy of wisdom and knowing that I experience in my being / mind as the being of light and clarity and truth that I know, as I hear these words, is clear and empty of any 'personal' energy, coming from a very high spiritual force.

You are heard.

May we walk together in Light and consciousness. May there be understanding between us. May there be union.

THE PLAN

In 2000 I heard:

Everything is known at the appointed time. There are no mistakes and nothing is lost. Every soul finds its way to God – the choice is just in the way, be it rough or smooth. These matters are appointed, chosen in the great mercy and compassion of the One, through the wisdom of each soul.

When I read this to my partner at the time, he asked, do we still have choice – then he sees that he is seeing the words in terms of an external God, instead of the inner God, inner divine, that I have been experiencing, that we both know and Love, and he then understands. We have the choice of our Hearts and the power inside us which guides us in alignment.

There are no mistakes and nothing is Lost

'NOTHING HAS GONE TO WASTE', My Father said as we walked in the precious wood, the holy wood they planted at the Millennium – When I first stood on the Christ point of this land I received a vision of the woodland as a huge temple of light. I was told it would take 50 years to reach it's power. I feel it is really sanctified ground.

I hear:

There is nothing which is not as I intended, nothing which is imperfect.

And as I hear this, I feel the power of trust growing in my heart.

And the pleasure of my two feet on the ground (always this, the essence, the foundation) moving forward, in tune with myself, one step at a time.

This feast of the now of Life.

Your powers are greater than you know.

ROLE

You can feel great fear of 'the role that is expected of you', forgetting that it is only my love, in the instant, that exists; your role is simply to live this.

Your self-deception is to impose a structure on this. The role of Christ / Buddha nature has no form save that which I choose – There is nothing to be expected or known beyond the totality of the instant. Your partner is to be totally released from the image you had of him – it is only by inhabiting yourself beyond the constructs of these roles and allowing him to do the same, that you experience true freedom in my Love. This is so for all your brothers and sisters.

There is nothing I require of you beloved daughter, save that you enter the silence as called to align your will to mine. You will be shown and will know the limits you are inhabiting.

ALL IS INTACT, REMEMBER THIS. It is essential, fundamental to your work, your joy, your harmony. (YOUR WORK IS YOUR JOY, YOUR HARMONY)

You have hidden your light for far too long – let your magnificence shine truly.

PEACE

The greatest need of the Human Soul

There is peace here on earth. It is growing.

    It is found in each human soul, deep in the recesses of the forgotten memories. The memories are of a time before birth, when you were at one with Me, held forever in my eternal embrace, as you are now, awakening to this fact, here on earth. This is a great time, a time of new understanding and growth; through you for all your brothers and sisters, who will celebrate. Rejoice now, through each breath of holy air into your system, rejoice and feel me near. I am uncovering you.

I am uncovering you in great peace and with care. Do not be afraid. The time of persecution is past. There will be misunderstandings and misconnections aplenty, and you are not to be discouraged by these growing pains. Find faith in your new brotherhood, the new understanding that reveals itself in relationships. You are being fed.

Peace, peace is the greatest fever. The greatest need of the human soul.

You have always known this, and it is revealed in your constant prayer to Me.

Peace is the source of all I am. Your longing for Me is your longing for Peace.

All shall be well when you as a race realise this.

Many have known this through the ages.

Turn more deeply to Me, in the silence. You are met. You carry this silence within you at all times, in the greatest freedom. You are close to me now, in freedom.

There is peace on earth. Find it in each soul, resonate with it, speak with it, touch it anew.

After Meditation, I hear:

There is great peace here, inside you. Carry it forth amongst your brothers and sisters, as you walk your daily life. You are coming Home, in every minute you are making this choice. Your will is aligned to mine, as it ever has been. Brother, sister, mother, father, they need your healing, give it to them, in the simplest encounters.

There is nothing to rush for.

Peace is Grace understanding itself, coming Home to itself.

It is the greatest need of the Human spirit. It is the greatest salve.

You do well to find this peace in the silence. It is the essence of your soul. You are a peace–bringer to this My realm, which sorely needs this balm at this time. You have nothing to fear. We are at the beginning, a time of no-place, no dimensions.

There is nothing that is other than Me, all is One. You have taught this through your life, though you have struggled with it on the inner planes. There is no way you can be separated from Me, with any thing other than your perception, which can be turned always towards unity and peace. Peace is understanding itself. It shall grow in you. Breathe into it now, and feel it spreading throughout your system. All is well.

Your ego is dissolving, moving through into greater love and understanding.

Their surrender is nigh, those who work against the human soul. It shall be achieved. And all shall be well. All is well, my child, my loved one.

Set your soul free to perform the love and commitment it was chosen to bring to this realm. You were chosen to bring the high energies of love and commitment to the divine through to this dense realm, as you have such great belief and commitment. Your energies of surrender to the truth are commended.

Go with Love, Go in complete faith and total trust. Go in Peace, all is in hand, and is well underway. Walk in total trust of my voice and of your eternal Light and its strength

CHAPTER SEVEN

CONCLUSION

Each moment is a new creation.

Through this journey of the Golden Road, through tuning in and listening, through sensing and growing, I have been blessed with a deep understanding of this and the other truths and awarenesses I have shared. There is this knowledge – that every moment is a new creation, a new opportunity to feel, think, see and know anew from a wiser perspective, a new possibility……. - there is this knowledge and there is also the space and presence which this calls forth into our experience. The life, the light, the opportunity.

In each moment, we can find ourselves anew
We can begin again.

Again and again, I enter the silence and find, when I need it, the Voice of the Golden Road. The Voice of Great Spirit, and the voices of all the angels and Beings of Light who walk with the highest good of all Beings in their hearts. In the silence, and with song in my heart, I travel on this path, following where I am guided, listening and giving thanks. Make space and time to connect inwardly, and listen if to the small still voice in the silence.

Be blessed. Know yourself anew. In God's hands, and heart – and, remember, it is endless this embrace. It continues forever, throughout and beyond time, and it is the silence and peace at the Centre of your being.

Be well now, as you take steps towards coming into a deeper listening and integration of wholeness.

This is indicative of profound change and a new opening to life and light. It is a coming into Truth, a new beginning and it is indeed recommended that you take these profound steps to a new life that you have seen and been supported towards.

All will fit into place and come at the appointed time, as you open your heart and move deeper into the truth and the understanding.

Go well now and rest in the arms of this warm loving night. Call the powers of change and transformation to you, open yourself to their energies.

Love yourself. Trust yourself and the uncovering of your heart's life.

At Millom circle, Cumbria, UK

And in this uncovering, I find: It is in the holy and wild places of the world that the core of my soul finds her place and is most deeply fed - in communion with the moon, the stars, the wind and the rain, the sun burning, the stones of ancient sacred sites, and the open shore of the sea.

I hear the birds, I answer their callings, I touch the trees, I listen.

This connection with, and my regular immersion into, the wildness of nature, and the energies I find therein, supports and strengthens my relationship with my soul and with Divine Guidance. It prepares my being, my vessel.

I reclaim this communion as vital and own my relationship to this Living intelligent planet and the Light at her heart as the very Centre of my life. The Earth mother, Gaia, is the living force of the Divine in this world, and it is my relationship with her that shapes and informs my understanding of all that is Sacred.

As I honour my relationship to the sustaining earth, I am reclaiming my relationship with a Living Spirit, the True Divine force.

Opening Wings

I can see further
than I thought I could,
can feel and hear
more deeply.

The earth turns
and the stars wheel,
here in the present,
this night.

I can see the edge of the land
and then the open sea.
I can hear the stars breathing

.

A thousand white birds land.
Their single beating heart
thuds in my chest.
I feel their love as my own,

in the endless sound
of their wings opening.

All is become.
All is blessed.

Thank you, I whisper

LIGHT:

To your heart, constantly, let the Light shine.   Let the Light stream forth unto your brothers and sisters and to all souls guided to you.

Let your Light lead the way only.

Let the future be revealed in the Light you show the world.

It is freedom, joy exceeding known limits.

*You are **shedding your man-made armour**, which is no longer appropriate for the age ahead. Bliss will be known in all you achieve. Let joy be the watchword for all you do. Let the colours fly, let the joy be known.*

Eternal rest in the beloved arms of God.

You have to know the strength of your own spirit, and its endless power.

The phase is completed – have faith.
I would have you know your own strength and know that you can always rest on it, always rely on it. It will not let you down beloved, nor will it leave you.

We need to breathe into our strength, which expands and becomes the strength and power of the whole cosmos.

I see that it has never gone away, has always been available, just in the silence off to the side of what might be busy life, as we breathe right in the centre of our beings.

Have patience with the process, the uncovering. Know that you are led.
You must heal yourself and become all you are, singing against the sky.
Faith is like a deep endless well of clear water.

Blessed is the truth, known in the footsteps you are taking.

This can be true for all of us. There is always truth and Light present as we form the steps towards our own unique, authentic pathways in life. The guidance we need will come to us all if we centre ourselves in the silence and tune into the peace off the Divine Essence we can find there. Follow your breath, and create the space in your life that you need.

Hear the voice inside you and listen as it guides.   Know the silence, and the power it contains.   Find your voice and Speak your Truth always.

Coming Through

We are all coming through and into
ourselves. Into the highest aspect of our selves.
We are growing, becoming. We are.

It is a great day
that has dawned, and the light
is pouring forth and on and into
our deepest places.

See yourself.

Let the light pour into your heart,
making all things possible.
Let the light pour forth from your heart
into this beautiful world.
Giving thanks, giving thanks.

Thank you, for all you are, for all you do.

See the beauty around and inside you, always.

The sun touches the damp grass,
and a blackbird calls. The sky
is becoming the clearest blue.

A song is rising in the world.

This song is a deep freedom, a coming through.

It is understanding. It is opening.

Listen now.

Breathe,

and know.

Please see more about my work

at

https://www.songofawakening.org.uk

I hope The Golden Road has brought you joy and inspiration, and that it will continue to do so.

THE GOLDEN ROAD

My Journey with Spirit

Printed in Great Britain
by Amazon

43601245R00063